INFLUENCER CEO

How to Use YOUR OWN Influence to
Easily Create and Build an Online Store:
A Foolproof, No Inventory, No
Advertising Method to Your First $100k

Gina L. Kershaw

INFLUENCER CEO

© 2018 Gina Kershaw
All rights reserved.
ISBN: 978-1-79326-830-3

No part of this publication may be reproduced, distributed, or transmitted in any form or by any means, including photocopying, recording, or other electronic or mechanical methods, without the prior written consent of the publisher, except in the case of brief quotations embodied in reviews and certain other non-commercial uses permitted by copyright law.

The following trademark is owned by Gina Kershaw: Influencer CEO™
While all attempts have been made to verify the information provided in this publication, neither the author nor the publisher assumes any responsibility for errors, omissions, or contrary interpretations on the subject matter herein.

This book is for entertainment purposes only. The views expressed are those of the author only and should not be taken as expert instruction or commands. The reader is responsible for his or her own actions.
The author has recommended several products and services in this book. !
Any products recommended in this book have been personally used and tested by the author. The reader or purchaser is advised to do their own research before making any purchases online.

Adherence to all applicable laws and regulations including international, federal, state, and local governing professional licensing, business practices, advertising, and all other aspects of doing business in the US, Canada or any other jurisdiction is the sole responsibility of the reader or purchaser. Neither the author nor the publisher assumes any responsibility or liability whatsoever on the behalf of the purchaser or reader of these materials.

DEDICATION

For my unbelievably talented children -
Erin, Paige, Rachel and Wyatt.
I hope you will always know you already have
everything you need
to create incredible and fulfilling lives.
Go for it.

TABLE OF CONTENTS

DEDICATION 5

TABLE OF CONTENTS 6

THIS BOOK IS FOR YOU IF 9

CRAZY LEAPS OF FAITH 13

YOU'VE COME THIS FAR, NOW WHAT? 21

FIRST THE FOUNDATION, AKA THE BUZZ 27

YOU HAVE A GIFT 33

ARE YOU MAKING ENOUGH MONEY TO PAY YOUR RENT? 39

FINANCE 101 FOR INFLUENCERS 45

THE SCARY WORD 51

MY GOAL 57

YOUR STORE. NO INVENTORY, NO SHIPPING, ... 61

NO ADVERTISING COSTS 61

GET IN THE CAR, BEAUTIFUL. LET'S GO SHOPPING! 67

DEFINE YOUR DEMOGRAPHIC – WHO IS YOUR FOLLOWER? 77

WHAT'S YOUR PASSION? LET'S FIND YOUR NICHE. 81

NAME YOUR STORE 85

THE FUN PART! 91

LASTLY 99

| LET'S CONNECT | 103 |
| WORK WITH ME | 104 |

"But maybe, if you put your disbelief aside, roll up your sleeves, take some risks, and totally go for it, you'll wake up one day and realize you're living the kind of life you used to be jealous of."

--Jen Sincero
You Are a Badass: How to Stop Doubting Your Greatness and Start Living an Awesome Life

THIS BOOK IS FOR YOU IF . . .

You are ready to roll up your sleeves and change your life.

In this book I am going to share a secret. Successful influencers and bloggers know it. Large influence marketing companies know it. But most influencers don't. You may not even understand the terms yet...

After reading this book you are going to have a new perspective, and you are going to start thinking about this secret. Nonstop. Because that's how great ideas work.

Of course, I'm not telling you anything new. When you started thinking about being an influencer or blogger, the ideas flowed like crazy. And you probably couldn't sleep or think about anything else.

Why do you think that happens?

It happens because when an idea takes up residence in your heart and mind, and you start to realize that this idea can have a huge impact on your lifestyle, your family, your home, your sanity, etc..., and your brain starts trying to figure out exactly how it can make it happen.

Then it keeps going and going until you either take steps forward, or let the idea go - intentionally or through inaction.

When the idea about working as an influencer came into your life, you decided to go for it.

You are making it happen!! You go girl!! Now you are taking the next steps to learn even more about what you can accomplish.

I am confident that as an entrepreneur, the wheels in your mind are going to start spinning until you make this happen. And it is going to Change. Your. Life.

This book is about how you become an Influencer CEO. It is a guide on "How to use your own influence to create a six-figure income and have the lifestyle you have always wanted."

It is time for you to be taken seriously.

It is time for you to take your business to the next level.

On the outside (what your followers see), your social media will be the way it has always been. You can keep up with all the ways you are building up your numbers, but you will also have a new game plan. By the way, the numbers don't really mean anything (but I think you already know that.)

This book is going to introduce a completely new concept to you. And….
You may initially feel like you do not have the skills to make it happen. I am
here to tell you that YOU DO.

You can easily take this secret and create a life that will be comfortable,
prosperous and freaking awesome. II will be here with you, all along the way.

We will take this step by step, and you are going to have the knowledge that
will take you where you always hoped you would be when you started this
journey. As you progress and grow with your business, you are going to find
success and abundance. You are ready for this, and the universe is ready to
give it to you.

You are going to achieve what you set out to achieve (although you did not
know how you were going to do it at the time you started…).

I have created an action plan for you to see how you can take this program
and easily get your first online store up and running. I am offering it as a free
gift to my readers. Just head on over to www.ginakershaw.com and check
out the downloads page.

As you learn and focus on how to build this business, you are going to love
what you can do. You are going to realize how amazing you really are. You
are going to be amazed at what is going to happen!

And as you become more and more successful, you are going to be able to
motivate and inspire others that are just behind you on the path.

It is time to master this business. It is time to become an Influencer CEO.

"There's a turning point. It arrives when we find ourselves quietly hovering inside the realization that the choice is between two pains: the pain of the jump or the pain of regret."

--Victoria Erickson

CRAZY LEAPS OF FAITH

I am just going to say it.

In order to make it big, you will have to get out of your comfort zone.

People that have made a difference in their own lives (and in the world) are the people that have taken risks and have gone after their dreams — even if there were people around them that tried to talk them down.

I can speak to the success of crazy leaps of faith. And ... also the naysayers.

I used to work as a criminal defense attorney. I had a secure six-figure annual income and plenty of education and titles to make me feel really important. But, something was missing.

Me. Insert epiphany here. I really didn't like my life that much. The work could be very interesting and worthwhile, but the daily hostile atmosphere sucked. I mean really, why do lawyers have to be such assholes? Disclaimer: most of the lawyers I worked with in the criminal courts were awesome! But the civil attorneys, well.... their egos entered the room before they did, and that didn't always sit well with me.

I had just spent the previous year of my career involved in four gang murder trials. I had defended my clients to the best of my ability and, damn, I was good at what I did. I took my job very seriously and worked hard for my clients. I knew that if I wanted to, I could excel in this profession and be the best in my field. But was that what I wanted?

I wasn't sure...

As I moved into my fifteenth year of practicing law and defending some of the worst criminals and predators around, I decided to stop and look at myself in the mirror. I had to accept this life (and be happy about it), or I had to make a drastic change.

I had to decide whether I could pay off my student loans or ... die broke and happy. Haha, not really. Well, kinda. (At least I thought so at the time).

I really did have to decide whether I was going to continue to be a slave to that six-figure income and prestige, or whether I was going to jump off the train, get humble, start again, and do something worthwhile.

I decided to start again. And I got humble(d) in the process. It was definitely hard at times because I had family that wanted me to keep working as a lawyer. I think they took some form of pleasure in saying that I was a lawyer. I get it. My dad was able to say – "Did you see my daughter in the news? She is a badass criminal defense attorney." He loved telling all of his friends about me. Can you relate? I can easily say he was devastated when I said no more.

This should probably be a heading, but ... you have to Live Your Own Life!!

The way to be successful now is so different from the way your parents experienced it. Trust your instincts and your own knowledge!

Soon after I left my job working as an indigent criminal defense attorney, I felt inspired to start a law practice focused on helping women. I had so many ideas!!

I absolutely loved the idea of working with and helping women. Even though my law practice for women did not eventually grow as I had hoped, looking back, I know it was an important step in my growth. It was the step I needed in order to learn my passion, which is helping other people to achieve their goals and to see the potential in themselves.

Really, there is so much potential in Every. Single. Person. Amen.

I took a HUGE (and crazy) leap of faith and turned my head towards good, positivity and creativity. The fancy car and big house had to go, but I was okay with simplifying.

It was a truly courageous moment in my life. I am grateful for a husband that didn't judge me and instead just loved me and encouraged me. I was finally free to find my true self. It has been such a fun journey since then!!

I retired from lawyering and started work in the retail industry. I went back to school and got my MBA in Marketing and Finance. I took a sabbatical from law and I found a place where I could experience the very best of management and the creative process. I was determined to become teachable and moldable, so I started at the very bottom of the business as a part-time sales associate making minimum wage. Yes… minimum wage. Hahaha. It was freaking wild.

Minimum wage was the bomb. I didn't have to prove anything. I was free to learn and grow without restraints.

I distinctly remember my interview – the General Manager asked me why I wanted to work for them. She offered me $10.00 an hour. At the time, I had been billing clients $350.00 an hour. It is crazy, but I just didn't care anymore. I wanted to learn.

She didn't realize that I needed the creativity and that I had a different motive. I would have done it for free (and at that rate, it basically was. LOL). I told her that I was ready for a change and that I just wanted to work in the retail/fashion industry – regardless of where I started.

Thank you Haleh. You will never know the gift you gave me when you took a chance and hired me.

I was there to learn everything I could about the business. It was almost like going to this high-level experiential school – and they paid for me for it! Winning!

And, of course, motivated people don't stay at the bottom very long.

Within two years I was part of a senior management team that was managing a $14 million/year business. In the process, I learned about the metrics of retail sales, how to successfully manage a large business, and, best of all, how to inspire and mentor others.

It was truly a gift – and I am so thankful.

A few years in, I realized that I had learned all that I could, and I knew that I had to move on and find the next best step.

So, I did.

By the way, <u>it is okay to move on</u>!!! And you should!!

You may be comfortable where you are now. You may be at the top of your game in the company that you are at, but change is how you constantly improve and grow. Please don't settle.

PLEASE DON'T SETTLE.

If you are at that place, you know what I mean. You are ready to move on. You are ready to claim your next victory.

Are you ready? I will help you get there.

I have always had an entrepreneurial mindset. I am sure you do too! That is how you have had the vision and mindset to place yourself as a role model and influencer.

When you are open to the abundance of the universe, you are given ideas. Sometimes they come faster than you can use them, but you know you are inspired. And, damn. Feeling inspired is one of the best endorphins ever. It is the ultimate high.

You know exactly what I mean. Your mind starts rolling fast onto checklists and action plans, and it is hard to sleep. You want to work on your ideas and projects, and you want to share your excitement and goals. You are grateful for inspiration and motivation, and try to make the best of them while they are strong and powerful in your mind.

After I took that crazy leap of faith, confirmation of my courage came. Amazing ideas and creativity started flowing back almost immediately.

I felt alive again.

Working in the retail industry turned into entrepreneurial thinking, and it got me thinking about how I could have my own retail business. I looked into having a brick and mortar store, and also explored e-commerce.

As part of that curiosity about starting an online retail e-commerce business, I discovered dropshipping. WOW. I learned how it works, and how it does not require inventory or other expensive overhead.

I was sold.

From there, I researched everything I could about opening an online shop, launched a few stores of my own, and realized the huge potential this type of business has.

For me. For you.

This business is especially a game-changer or influencers who already have a solid following. You are the ones that are going to kill this. Because you can do it without paying for ads, and that, my friend, is the ultimate game.

"If you are insecure, guess what? The rest of the world is, too. Do not overestimate the competition and underestimate yourself. You are better than you think."

--Tim Ferriss
Bestselling Author of *The 4-hour Workweek.*

YOU'VE COME THIS FAR, NOW WHAT?

You have people who want to hear your voice.

They look forward to reading your latest post, seeing your latest photo, or following you around the world as you visit new and interesting places.

Your followers look forward to having you as a part of their lives because you are interesting, intelligent, funny, authentic, relevant, and an image of who they would like to be. You have the power to really influence people to make positive changes in their lives. You are amazing!

Now that you have reached this level, you may be asking yourself how you can leverage that influence to reach a higher peak of success than you already have.

Of course, if attending NYFW, being invited to awesome parties, and getting free stuff is what your goal was, you can stop here. You made it!

But ... I think you want more.

You want something more than just waiting around for businesses to notice you and contact you.

You want to be proactive and to make your own success.

You want a solid income.

You want to be taken seriously.

You want this business to be what takes you and your family to a higher wealth level.

You want to contribute meaningfully to your family.

You want to be an example to your children.

You want to become everything you were meant to be!

Come along with me. Let me show you how you can build this business and have the lifestyle you always wanted.

This book is going to help you:

1. Build your business smart.
2. Make intelligent decisions regarding the structure and system of your business.
3. Leverage your own influence and follower engagement to have a steady income
4. Diversify your business so that you can be making money 24 hours a day, 365 days a year.
5. Have more balance in your life.

6. Work less and make more money.
7. Become a true business mogul.

You can do it! There is a way.

Can I start with this idea? YOU HAVE ALREADY PROVEN YOURSELF!

In the words of Jen Sincero, "You are totally a bad ass."

Believe it, sister.

You may have started this business as a hobby, with the dreams of someday making it into something you can live off of. You probably didn't initially realize how much work it was going to be, but as your blog or Instagram account has taken off, you have seen the potential that is there, and you love it.

But, you have also wondered if you really have what it takes, and you have questioned yourself and your abilities.

You have to read this book through the eyes of someone who can see their true potential. Read it and think of where you can be six months from now.

Visualize yourself quitting the 9 to 5 and running your business as the CEO. See yourself traveling and enjoying life a bit more. See yourself not worrying about money and paying the bills. See yourself as someone who can be as generous as they want. See yourself mentoring and helping other influencers stabilize their business models too.

Now feel how rewarding your life is. This is what you can have.

You can do this.

It is definitely not easy, but it is not hard either! You just have to be willing to trust and believe in yourself.

Look where you have come from. Look what you have accomplished. Do you even realize how many people look up to you and want to hear your voice? Check your number of followers. That should give you a good idea. I bet there are even more people than that.

You have proven that you are a leader - in fashion, in style, in fitness, in wellness, in mothering, etc.... whatever your platform is. And people trust you.

This is key.

Are you ready? Let's start with a few business basics.

"Nothing influences people more than a recommendation from a trusted friend."

--Mark Zuckerberg
Founder and CEO of Facebook

FIRST THE FOUNDATION, AKA THE BUZZ

In marketing, the absolute best advertising is word of mouth, or "buzz." Marketers and ad agencies do everything they possibly can to generate this buzz. It is golden.

The reason that buzz is the best type of marketing is pretty clear. The simplest way to explain buzz is that people trust a product if their friends are using it. This makes sense. If your friend suggests a product - or even if they just acknowledge that they use it - you are more likely to find it and buy it. Done. End of story.

It starts very simply. People start talking about something – it could be a book, a movie, or a new product. They may just mention it to their best friend over coffee, they might wear it or use it around other people. They may even share it over social media.

When the right people (people with influence) start talking about it, a few things happen.

First, an excitement builds because the person talking about it is excited enough to share how much they love it. The person hearing this excitement goes right out to see that movie or buy that product because they don't want to miss out. Then, the next person shares their excitement about the product. This is how things go viral.

It can happen very quickly if enough people are hearing and sharing.

Advertisers have known for years that if they can get buzz on their product, they have it made! Once word-of-mouth promotion starts, it becomes free advertising. Not only that, but now there is social proof that the product is worth buying.

Think about it.

When you know that your friend has bought something, and they <u>love it</u> and want to share their delight with you, you have the best social proof. You are willing to buy because someone else already has.

No one wants to be first, but they are more than willing to be second. They absolutely do not want to miss out on the latest thing. FOMO is real, people. (Especially in this business).

I'm sure you have seen how this happens.

Do you remember the movie Napoleon Dynamite? Well, you probably shouldn't. That movie was an obscure indie film that didn't have a single famous actor. With a budget of only $400,000, Napoleon Dynamite was given a limited release, and was destined for home video. But an incredible thing happened. People started talking about it and its quirkiness.

They started quoting the film.

Word-of-mouth buzz got people out to see this movie over and over again. Napoleon Dynamite pulled in $46 million and became a pop culture phenomenon.

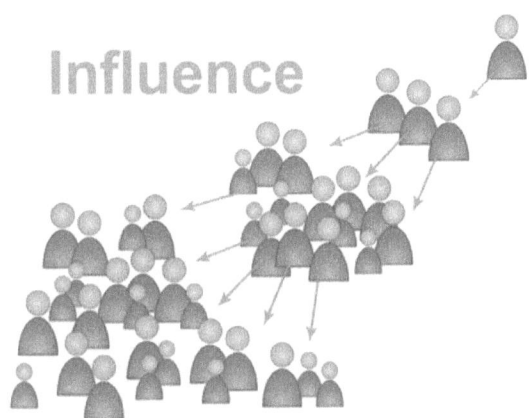

This is the power of "the buzz." It is a real phenomenon – and even more visible these days when we can see just how many people are viewing and responding to products and videos. When you look at an advertisement, do you consider how many people have viewed it, liked it, or shared it? Of course, you do!!

You may even be willing to share it yourself based upon these metrics.

I am not saying that you will only share it if lots of people are sharing, but… subconsciously you know that your share will be more accepted because it has already been shared.

We are sharing so much of ourselves, while simultaneously still trying to people-please. We are posting the pictures that present us in the best light (literally). Social proof of a post – (lots of other people viewing and sharing it) gives us permission to share too – without worry that we are stepping outside the social acceptance circle.

ENTER INFLUENCER MARKETING.

This influencer path you have chosen really is amazing. It has taken businesses and ad agencies completely by surprise. The ones that touted the "buzz" as the greatest marketing tool a product can have are only recently opening their eyes to what influencers can do.

When you have a solid following (think engagement, not numbers) you can have an incredible effect on a business.

When you put your seal of approval on something, you give it social proof and the "buzz" happens. What ad agencies have been trying to create for years, you have in your hand. It is so simple, yet so freaking awesome.

It is a real thing. YOU have this power! You may not even realize the power you have, and that is why I am here to tell you. As an influencer, you have the power to generate this buzz.

So go out there and use it to your benefit. If you love something and feel good endorsing it – do it! The more good things that we can experience and buy, the better! The more you can share and give your seal of approval to, the more people will trust you.

Of course, remember that your recommendation has to always be authentic and real. It has to stay trustworthy. You wouldn't tell your friends to go see a movie you hated, right? They would not ask for your recommendation again.

Remember… if they trust you, <u>they will also share what you recommend</u>. Where it goes from there can be life-changing.

"Be who God meant you to be and you will set the world on fire."

--St. Catherine of Siena

YOU HAVE A GIFT

You are constantly going and doing and accomplishing.

You are driven and willing to work hard.

You believe in yourself and the creative process.

You have faith in the universe and realize that everything you have ever wanted is right here, waiting for you to pick it up.

You are a rock star!

Good! That's awesome!

However, with this gift, you have also realized that you want more from life, more from business, more from relationships. There is nothing wrong with wanting more – this is how we progress and grow in life.

And you have never wanted to be stagnant.

In order to reach out and to develop your unique self and obtain more from life, you have started this amazing journey.

Right now, you may feel like it is hard to get ahead in this business and that you are just one of millions. But the best part of your journey as an influencer or blogger is that it is totally based upon the uniqueness of YOU. There is only one you in the universe. One.

The people that will listen to you and follow you will do it because they want to hear your unique voice.

There is no competition here – only abundance. Lots of abundance. There is more than enough for you and every other influencer out there.

If you are willing to let your true self show through, your voice will resonate with other people who need you.

Never doubt this great gift. You only have to be willing to share yourself – this includes your struggles and your faults along with all of the good stuff.

When you are your own original self, you will help others who may be on a similar life path.

- You will inspire and motivate.
- You will make a difference.
- You will change lives and your own in the process.

All of this becomes important when you consider your next steps. The fact that you have a rare and individual voice, and that your followers want to hear that voice, gives you incredible power. You already have what it takes. You will not have to pay for advertising or go into any kind of debt.

You already have the leverage. That leverage is invaluable.

By using the influence you already possess, you will be able to sell products and ideas that are uniquely your own. You will be able to put your own seal of approval on products that you will personally select, try, and sell from your own store.

Do you understand the power of your seal of approval? It helps start the buzz that we talked about in the last chapter.

<u>This is the entire reason businesses want influencers working for them</u>.

When you post something good about a business or their product, it gives it that very necessary "social proof."

When you say "Hey – I LOVE this – you should try it," the business you are promoting has started a word-of-mouth campaign. As a marketer, you should realize that a word-of-mouth campaign is a totally BALLS OUT campaign. This business is banking on you and your influence.

When you say that their product is cool — how many of your followers are going to try it? A LOT. Yes. A LOT. Even if they don't try it, they are going to tell their friends about it.

Businesses know what they are doing.

You may feel like your influence is not worth very much — so you may promote a product or service for a minimal fee or for free gifts. But, the truth is that this advertising may be THE BEST advertising they have planned — and they aren't even really paying for it.

I am going to digress for a moment — but this really makes me crazy!!

When I was a full-time attorney, I used to pay $2,000 <u>a month</u> to advertise in the Yellow Pages. Hell, you may not even know what the Yellow Pages are — they are that archaic. Basically it was a big freaking book full of phone numbers where someone could look up attorneys alphabetically. At the time, if you were not in the Yellow Pages, your potential clients could not find you. (No internet, obvi).

The point is… $ 2,000. A. Month.

To advertise.

Hoping that someone may see the ad and decide to call.

If you really think about it, the only reason any person would EVER turn to the Yellow Pages to find an attorney would be because <u>they had no idea who to call</u>!! If their best friend, or someone they trusted, recommended an attorney, they would never even open that damn book. They would go with the recommendation. Makes sense, right?

YOU ARE THE FREAKING RECOMMENDATION.

Do you even realize how valuable that is?

Before we dive in, I just want to talk to you about something.

You may be thinking you do not have the skills to set a successful influencer business up – and you may also be wondering how it works.

I promise I will guide you through and help you to understand and to set this system up for yourself. It will be easier than you think. You have what is takes. You just need a small step of courage to get you out of your comfort zone and into this place where you will SHINE!

"The true entrepreneur is a doer, not a dreamer."

--Nolan Bushnell

ARE YOU MAKING ENOUGH MONEY TO PAY YOUR RENT?

By becoming an influencer, you have taken a step that many people are afraid to take. For whatever reason, they are unsure about who they are and whether people will want to see and hear them.

In order to become an influencer, you have to believe in yourself.

You are doing it!

I LOVE IT!!

I know it takes courage, and courage is the only thing that will ever get you what you want. You have to be able to step out of your current situation to get into the next one.

I applaud you! I am cheering for you!

By taking this step, you are showing yourself and the universe that you are ready for success, ready for abundance, and ready to live your best life.

You started at the beginning (by the way, everyone starts here, even influencers with millions of followers). You had a single follower, maybe your mom or your best friend, but since then you have built your brand by researching, writing, and looking for ways that you could personally help people, and the followers started following.

Now you are in a place where you have brought relevant and interesting information about fashion, fitness, business, life, etc. to lots of people who find your social media and blog worthwhile. You are meticulous about curating your photo wall and you take pride in the content you are providing. You know you are making it happen.

Then you had a "what next?" moment.

You doubted yourself and your ideas. You looked at yourself and thought, "Why isn't this working?" ... "Why can't I get businesses to contact me?" ... "Why can't I make consistent money from my Instagram?"

You may have even felt like a fraud, wondering why you ever thought you could be an influencer.

If this has happened to you, you are definitely not alone!! Dismiss those crazy, negative thoughts from your head!

You may have tried to move forward by seeking information on how to "monetize" your Instagram following, but have not found the formula for the success you have dreamed of.

You tried blog posts, books and classes about how to reach out to businesses so that you can promote their products, get free stuff, and make some money. These resources gave you some ideas about how to connect with businesses and companies to make money, but you still have doubts about where this journey will take you.

The fact is that most influencers are willing to promote a product by sharing a picture, a story, an IGTV for nothing more than exposure.

They believe that if they promote a product they love (for free), they will get more followers from the post of the product and the story, which will then lead to more opportunities.

This is partly true – if all you want is free deodorant for the rest of your life.

I want more for you.

There is definitely a way to monetize your Instagram or blog. That should certainly be part of your business model. But not the only part.

Only a small percentage of influencers and bloggers actually make the kind of money that gives them a life! Those individuals are doing more than just monetizing. Remember that only a few (that monetize only) actually make enough money to make a difference in their household budget.

Let's be real. The reason you got into this game is because you want to make money.

So exactly how much have you made?

Have you made enough money to "stick it to the man?" (Love that movie, haha).

Are you making enough to quit your 9 to 5 and travel the world?

Or, are you down to the basics?

Are you making enough to cover rent, your car payment and groceries?

And…. If you don't have to pay rent or a mortgage, are you at least bringing in a few extra dollars so that you can hit happy hour every weekend with your friends? C'mon now.

Studies done on the habits of influencers show that most influencers don't get paid anything to promote a product. That is because most are more than willing to promote a product if they get one (or more) for free.

<u>This is a windfall for businesses</u>.

In addition, because there are so many willing to promote a product for free, the only ones really getting paid are the influencers and stylists that have HUGE followings. (Maybe 3% of all influencers/bloggers out there).

There is a better way. It is more than monetizing.

I am talking about getting real, starting a freaking awesome business, running your own company like the badass that you are, and making money. Lots of money. If you just want to take pictures and promote someone else's product, this book is NOT for you. No judgements here. Maybe you are fine with where you are at, and if you get a sponsored post 3-4 times a month, you are good to go. That is totally up to you.

But, if you want more ... and you are willing to try something new... Let's do it! Let's create something awesome. Let's rock your world! I want you to knock it out of the park!

I want you to be able to live life on another level.

I want you to have freedom.

I want you to have options.

I want you to be able to employ other people and give <u>them</u> options.

I want you to live a life better than you imagined when you started this journey.

Please don't settle for what other influencers are doing. You can do – and have – so much more.

"The beautiful thing about learning is that nobody can take it away from you."

-- B.B. King

FINANCE 101 FOR INFLUENCERS

How much do you know about this business you are in?

Do you understand how brands look at you? If you have 50k followers or less, you are considered a <u>micro-influencer</u>. If you have 50k-100k followers, you fall into the <u>power-middle influencer</u> group. If you are in either of these groups, companies and brands are less likely to offer you long-term contracts.

The amount of money you can earn will depend on the number of engaged followers you have, and the going rate is about $100 per 10k followers. So, if you have a solid following of about 35k followers, you may be able to get $350 for an Instagram post.

... Although it is more likely that you will be offered about $350 in products. Which can be a good start.

Of course, you can't pay your rent on that kind of income – unless you are working your ass off 24/7 and taking everything that comes your way.

If you are taking everything that comes your way, you lose the voice that big brands are looking for. It's kind of a catch-22. Should you or shouldn't you? Sigh. And so you decide to post something based upon whether or not you have money to make your car payment this month.

That is not a good reason, sister.

By the way, did I mention that the entire point of this book is to give you enough income so that you have freedom and options? If you are working non-stop and constantly have your face in your phone, you are not living your best life. There is so much more out there for you.

Here comes the Finance lesson.

Have you ever heard the phrase, "Don't put all your eggs in one basket?" Well, the reason you don't put all your eggs in one basket is because if the basket breaks, you're screwed.

In the financial world, they call this diversification.

This is a word that you need to know. <u>Diversification</u>.

When you diversify, you put your eggs in different baskets so that if one breaks, you still have another. If you are investing your money, you buy stocks and bonds instead of only stocks.

For example, if you put all of your savings into one company (like an airline), and that company went bankrupt because its planes were crashing, you would lose everything.

When you diversify you would buy stock in the airline, a tech company, some real estate, and some treasury bonds, so that no matter what, your money would still be safe if something happened to one of your other investments. It is that simple.

Why does this matter to you as a micro-influencer?

Because you need to diversify <u>your business</u> so that you always have a profitable angle.

You need to have more than one source of revenue just in case you have a slow month making money for posts and getting free products. If this happens, you will have another source of income.

When you diversify, you will have a more stable and steadier stream of income, and you will have less of a rollercoaster every month. You won't have to accept promotions that are off brand for your style just because you have to pay your gas bill. You will be able to organize your business in a way that will allow you more time to really work on the areas of your business that you want to work on.

Freedom and options, baby.

The bottom line is that if you are a micro-influencer, you are going to need a secondary way to monetize your influence so that you are not relying on little-known brands and shops to pay your bills every month (especially if you want to quit the 9-5 job you have).

When you set up this secondary income, you will diversify your business, and start acting like the bad ass business owner you really are.

If you are genuinely serious about having your own business, you need to know how to run it like a real business. And running a real business means that you are smart about where you put your energy (and your eggs).

When you have at least two sources of income for your Influencer business, you will see a higher return for your efforts, a more balanced life, and you may surprise yourself by making a freaking ton of money.

How bad do you want it? What is your why?

Diversifying is not hard — it just takes some smarts — and an entrepreneurial mindset.

Which <u>you have</u>.

Now that you understand what diversification is, you are already a huge step ahead. Every influencer should be doing it – but especially the micro-influencers because they are the ones that need the most stability as they build their business model.

Let me show you how.

"Man's mind, once stretched by a new idea, never regains its original dimensions."

--Oliver Wendell Holmes

THE SCARY WORD

E-commerce.

What the hell is e-commerce? Stay with me here.

There are two types of stores. The first is the old school type of store that you actually walk into. This is called a brick and mortar store. The second type of store is the one you visit from your computer. The is called an online store. The way that an online store sells to you is through e-commerce.

Even if you have never had your own e-commerce store, you have definitely shopped one. I would venture to say that every single person that is reading this book has shopped online. Yes, you have.

So…. You know that e-commerce is a thing. There are people and businesses making crazy money from it. But there is a HUGE difference between stores you have shopped online and the store that YOU are going to have. Those shops pay for advertising. They pay A LOT for advertising.

… You are not going to pay for advertising at all.

Did you catch that? You are not going to pay for advertising AT ALL.

This is the secret. You are going to learn how to do this using YOUR OWN influence. It is freaking amazing. I can't wait to see what you will do!

I will teach you how to do something that is going to put you leagues ahead of all of the other micro-influencers out there. You are going to get ahead because you are taking action. You are learning it and doing it.

There is no competition here – there is more than enough for EVERY INFLUENCER out there.

You are not only going to be at the start of the pack. You are going to lead the game.

Hopefully you will be an inspiration to other influencers and bloggers out there so that they can take their business to the next level too!

Even if you have never thought about having your own e-commerce shop (and may not even have known what e-commerce is before now), your life is about to be rocked!

If you are ready to up your game, take your business to the next level, be taken seriously as a business woman, and if you are ready to make a ton of money (without paying for advertising), you are definitely in the right place.

In this book I am going to show you a secret that is working for serious influencers. These influencers/bloggers have taken their influence to a completely new point where they can personally benefit from their own promotions, and they are making a ton of money (think, Kylie Jenner).

Really, you are already doing it for other businesses – why not yourself?

If you are ready to become the CEO of your own business, you can do it. Easily.

Everything you need to know will be given to you in this book – from the basics all the way to how to pick and launch a product.

You can do this!! There is really no time to waste – you can get ahead of this curve and be the one that sets the standard. Let me take you there!

In this book I've drawn on my own education and experience with e-commerce, fashion and social media. My background is in law and I have advanced degrees in Finance and Marketing.

In the past few years I have discovered a new passion for fashion, creativity, mentoring and coaching – and I absolutely love helping people find the inspiration and motivation to make their dreams come true.

Here's the bottom line.

When you have a thriving business you have success, wealth, freedom and options. You can work from home or travel. You can either be super busy or you can run your business on 2 days a week.

The point is, YOU choose.

Money will give you that freedom, and because you are an influencer already, you have the foundation you need to build, and build big!

If you are someone who wants to make a positive change in your life and have a big change in your financial situation… what is holding you back?

"One reason so few of us achieve what we truly want is that we never direct our focus; we never concentrate our power. Most people dabble their way through life, never deciding to master anything in particular."

--Tony Robbins

MY GOAL

My goal is pretty simple – to give you the right information, in the right order, that can help you to understand how to build an online store and then how to promote it without spending money on advertising.

My goal is to help get you to the next level – to make sure that you understand this business from the foundation up - taking years of struggling or stress out of the mix. With the right information you will see how easy it is to create a six-figure income.

You can decide how big you want it to get from there.

Influencers are entrepreneurial women (and men) with great ideas. They have a great work ethic. The thing that they lack most is the confidence to step outside their comfort zone and do something new. They are unsure what the next step may be, and sometimes they are not sure if they can figure it out and make it work!

My goal is to offer bloggers and influencers a shortcut, so you can avoid confusion and overwhelm, and instead enjoy a faster path to crazy success.

I'll show you:

- The newest way to use the influence you have built.
- What an e-commerce shop can do for your business (and life).
- How to easily start your own store without borrowing money or going into debt.
- How to find and test the right products.
- How to run your online store without holding any inventory or having to ship anything.
- How and promote your products through your own influence and collaborations (no advertising costs!)

And much more! Are you ready to change your life? (I hope so!) Keep reading!

"And here's the big news if you haven't figured it out already: when you do business online, you are open 24 hours a day, 7 days a week, 365 days a year. Your doors to business are always open and the idea of making money when you sleep is maybe not so far-fetched anymore. . . . it happens to me almost every night when I'm sleeping and a multitude of other entrepreneurs that are doing business successfully online as well."

--Chris Ducker
Youpreneur.com Founder

YOUR STORE. NO INVENTORY, NO SHIPPING, NO ADVERTISING COSTS

I'm guessing that at one point during this influencer journey you have thought about opening a store. I know this because you have an entrepreneurial mindset, and that is just what happens.

You had an awesome idea - and believed in yourself enough to know that other people would be interested in your products. You dreamed of this store and the creative fulfillment and freedom you would get from it, but you didn't know how to make it happen.

When it got down to the nitty-gritty, you realized that you would have to come up with money to buy stuff. You would have to buy and store inventory. You would need capital for a retail space and marketing.

You had the good idea - just not the bankroll. And then the idea quietly faded. It never died - it was still there always waiting for an opening - but without a rich grandma funding the project, you knew it was unlikely to happen.

Enter dropshipping.

This is going to change your life.

I am going to assume that you have never heard of dropshipping. Don't worry - most people haven't. But dropshipping is what is going to give you the edge.

This is what is going to give you the six or seven figure income you are ready for.

This is how you will feed your entrepreneurial desires.

This is how you are going to set yourself up as a Bad Ass Influencer CEO and have the successful business you have been dreaming about since you could remember.

Here we go!

<u>Dropshipping 101. The basic basics.</u>

-You have an e-commerce website.
-You sell things that you choose, test and believe in.
-Someone else holds the inventory.
-They ship it to your customer when a purchase is made.
-You pay less for the product than the price you sell it for.
-You keep the difference (the profit).

Make sense?
I know it sounds easy - and it is!! The hardest part of dropshipping is usually the marketing, but … you have that already. You are the marketing. Damn.

Let's look at how this works in a little more detail.

Let's say you are a Blogger/Influencer with about 10k followers. (I know this is low, but I want to show you how it works).

1. You create an e-commerce (online) storefront. You pick the name and design, You make sure branding is on point.
2. You create the actual store using an e-commerce site like Shopify. The themes (even the free ones) are beautiful and easy to create. This takes all of the guesswork out. There is also a free trial period to test it without any financial commitment.
3. You pick products that you think will resonate with your followers. You test them yourself to make sure they will work (plus… just a side note … when you use the product yourself you can sell it better. Think of things you own that you have recommended to friends.) It is hard to genuinely recommend something you have never seen, felt or tried.
4. You put the best products on your e-commerce website.
5. You recommend the product on your own social media platform (doing what other businesses have paid you to do).
6. You bring traffic to your own e-commerce website and sell the product.

Here's where it gets fun.

Example:

The price you pay for the product (cost)	$5.00
Estimated shipping costs	$2.00
Total out-of-pocket cost	$7.00

The price you sell the product for	$21.00
Your profit	$14.00

With a 2% conversion rate (only 2% of your followers buy the product) = 200 followers

200 people buy your product	@ $14.00 profit/each	$2,800 total profit

Let's say you have 50k followers with the same 2% conversion rate:

1000 people buy your product	@ $14.00 profit/each	$14,000 total profit

Do you see the potential? Crazy, right?!

All of this without borrowing from Grandma or even spending a single penny in advertising.

Best of all, with dropshipping, you never have to store any inventory or ship to any customers. You just manage the website and make sure you place the orders with your supplier.

This is the power you have.

I know many of you have a much larger following than the one I have used as an example, and this is for only one product. You have already set yourself up to be incredibly profitable!

I know it might be hard to believe you can achieve success and prosperity by building a dropshipping business. It's okay if you don't think you can do it on your own yet. Let me walk you through it and show you just how easy it really is.

"Online shopping . . . Because it's frowned upon to be in a store with no bra, sweatpants, and a glass of wine."

GET IN THE CAR, BEAUTIFUL. LET'S GO SHOPPING!

Now that you have a basic understanding of what dropshipping is, you are going to actually see how it works for yourself. You are going do something right now that most other influencers don't even know about.

You may be worried that you are not that tech-savvy and that you will not be able to figure this out. You can! I will walk you through the process step-by-step. You can always refer to these steps as you work on the action plan for today.

You are going to find that you are freaking awesome and that you can do anything if you set your mind to it!

Every dream or goal has steps - and this is just the very first one. You are already on your way to becoming a successful and accomplished business owner. You should be so proud of yourself!

You have learned about diversification and dropshipping! You are already way ahead of the game.

Now the fun part - let's go shopping.

There are a lot of companies that offer products at a wholesale price. As you go deeper into product searching, you can look at other companies (whether from China or the US). Right now, for the sake of simplicity, we are going to focus on the largest worldwide supplier.

You are going to open an AliExpress account, and I am going to show you, step-by-step.

It will be helpful for you to open your computer at this point and actually do the work while reading this. It will make more sense if you can see how it works in real time.

Open the AliExpress website by going to www.aliexpress.com. Then click on the "Join" button to get started.

After you click "Join," you will be taken to a page where you can enter your email address, name and password. Remember to use the email address that you want to connect to your store as this will be the email address that you use to connect your store to AliExpress in the future.

Go to the AliExpress Homepage - or if you wait just a moment it will take you there automatically.

That's it! So easy!

Your homework: Explore.

There are categories and subcategories. Find the ones that you are most interested in and look around a bit. Explore the nooks and crannies. Make a list of products that you might want to test out. Isn't this site great?

After you look around and get comfortable with the website, you may start to feel a little overwhelmed. Don't worry!

When you decide which products you would like to start with, you will be picking just a few and testing them out yourself first.

The goal right now is just to be curious. Don't think about which products you are ultimately going to put in your store. Just get comfortable wandering around the site, learning how the products are organized, and jotting down a few notes about the ones that grabbed your attention.

If you already enjoy internet shopping - you should be having fun! And... those prices!! Yep. They are real. This is how you make the big money.

As you are browsing AliExpress, you should be looking at products that you are naturally drawn to.

You should also be asking yourself - does this solve a problem for my followers/customers? Will any of these products bring value to them?

As you use AliExpress more often and become experienced at picking profitable products, you will see how important the marketing part of it is.

If the product is interesting enough to pique your customer's attention and if it can solve a problem for them, just add on your influencer seal of approval and you will have a sale.

Remember that buying something can be an emotional experience for the purchaser. A simple water bottle may be only worth $5 at a grocery store, but that same water bottle may be worth $25 when the purchaser remembers the picture you took in a flower field holding the bottle. She will always have a sweet emotional experience when she uses the same water bottle that you have. That is why your attachment and use of the products is so valuable.

Let's look at a sample product so that you will know what else to look for:

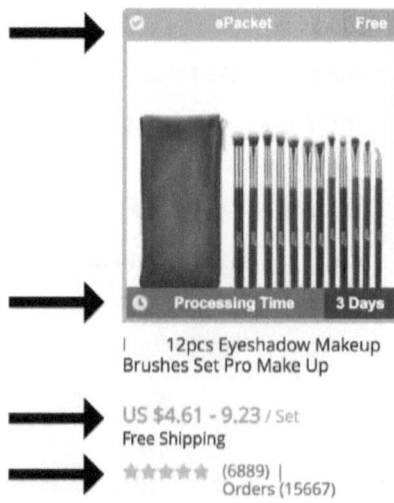

As you browse around, there are a few basic things that you will need to watch for:

> e-Packet: This means that the supplier uses an e-packet for shipping (and for this example, the shipping is actually FREE). This is the fastest way to have your product shipped to your customer. You don't want them waiting 3 months to get make-up brushes do you? When you are ordering products from China, the biggest complaint will usually be shipping time. Your solution is to ship the fastest (and cheapest) way you can. Welcome to e-packet. If the product you love does not have e-packet available, skip over it - it is just not worth it.

> Processing Time: Processing time is how long it takes for this supplier to process your order and ship it out to your customer. In this example, 3 days is stellar.

> Price: How much is this product, and how much do you think you would be willing to pay if you found this product in a store? (Always think about how much YOU would be willing to pay for something - after all, you are the best indication of your customer). Here, the brush set is $5.27 and the brush set plus the bag is $9.23. If you just bought the brush set, you

could potentially sell it for $17.99. Then, you could add-on the brush bag by suggesting an additional product. You are already making over $12 on this one item alone. Genius!!

➢ Stars: Do customers love it? This product has 6889 reviews and five stars. This is a good indication that customers are happy with this product.

If you click on the product, another screen comes up:

The column on the left shows some of the available photos you can use to market this product. These are a good start, and you can start your store using just the photos from AliExpress.

As we discussed, however, the best way to market a product is to test it yourself, take some of your own photos, and/or make a short video showing how the product is used. This makes the product real to your customers and they will be more likely to give it a try!

Take a look at the right of this figure to check on shipping. There is a drop-down arrow where you can see all the different shipping selections. Make sure this is on "e-packet" to get the best idea of when the product will reach your customer.

Feel good about using AliExpress?

When you pick a good product, you can feel good about promoting it, and you can make a lot of money by buying low and selling at a reasonable price.

Remember! <u>You have an edge here</u>!

Your followers are there for a reason. They believe in you. They want to be like you. That is why influencer marketing is so valuable. When you promote a product, it immediately takes away a layer of uncertainty for them. You have placed your seal of approval on a product. Your friends and followers trust you and YOU like the product, so why shouldn't they?

Remember! Business owners build entire marketing budgets around trying to get this type of buzz.

You have it at your fingertips.

REAL LIFE EXAMPLE:

The other day I got an email promoting an Influencer/Blogger Event. I happen to love this company, and I opened the email to find out about the latest event they were promoting. As part of the information about the event, this company included a blog post about how to take awesome photos. I was intrigued, so I opened the link to find out what I could learn.

I LOVE what I found in this blog post. I not only got some great info about how to take a compelling photo, but I could also click on a few products that would help me. I was completely sucked in.

I clicked on the first photo (an adorable pink polaroid camera).

Wait a second, here.

I immediately recognized the website I had been brought to as a dropship business. It was a cute website, and I landed on the page where I could "BUY NOW."

Validation. YES! An influencer (not only an influencer, but an influencer promotion company) was utilizing dropshipping. I could not wait to follow this post and see what happened.

The next morning, as I expected, I clicked on the cute little camera again, and guess what? SOLD OUT. Yep. This is the incredible power you have literally at your fingertips.

Now it is your turn.

Use this leverage to build a business, have more freedom, travel the world, whatever you want!! You can run an influencer business from anywhere. You can also run a dropshipping business from anywhere.

Go follow those dreams – use your influence to its full potential - and you can find YOUR true potential.

"If you try to help everyone, you'll never help anyone … You need to target."

--Steve Eakin
Founder of Startup Black Belt

DEFINE YOUR DEMOGRAPHIC – WHO IS YOUR FOLLOWER?

When you set up your Instagram account, you had a certain theme in mind. You may have decided to go with a fitness account, a lifestyle account, or a fashion account. You may have set up a blog and started writing. Maybe you picked a certain demographic, or maybe you just started by writing about things you love.

Either way, a certain group of people became interested in you. They started following you to see your photos and to hear what you had to say. If they stayed, they believed in you and wanted to hear your voice. This is your tribe.

Can you define this group of people?

Can you define a single member of this group that would be your perfect customer?

You may have heard the term "avatar." In business, an avatar is your ideal customer. This is the person that you are directing your business (and your IG) at. This avatar needs to become real to you. They need a name and you need to be able to describe everything about them.

For example:

If you run a lifestyle blog for Moms your avatar could be described like this:

Her name is Emily. She is 28 and has two children, ages 4 and 6. She is a stay-at-home mom that loves everything about mom-hood, except the occasional long nights and laundry. She is part of a rocking mom squad that works out together at the gym while their kids are being watched by the gym babysitting crew. Sometimes she takes her kids into the gym just for the babysitting and then sits for an hour and a half at the smoothie bar enjoying a few moments alone or with friends. She loves to cook and enjoys finding new recipes she can share. She loves fashion but wants to be able to find great deals. She loves authenticity but finds it sometimes difficult to express her own true self. She wants her husband to find her sexy. She values loyalty and love in both friends and family. She always wants to be in on the latest and greatest.

Can you get a feel for who Emily really is?

Homework: Create your avatar.

Be sure you name her/him. They are a real person and you have to see them that way.

Your avatar is who you are reaching out to. When you look at products and create posts, ask yourself if your avatar would enjoy and value what you have to offer. The more consistent you are, the better your business is going to be.

Your niche and your avatar will guide the type of store that you build, so it is very important that you know who you are reaching out to.

"Very narrow areas of expertise can be very productive. Develop your own profile. Develop your own niche."

--Leigh Steinberg
Successful Sports Agent and Author

WHAT'S YOUR PASSION? LET'S FIND YOUR NICHE.

As you have explored AliExpress, you have developed an idea of the kinds of products you are interested in. You have been drawn to certain types - and you may have even bought a few. This is great!

Today you are going to identify your niche. This is the area that you are going to focus on for your dropshipping business. It is very important that you take some thought to decide on your niche because you want it to be consistent with who you are, who your avatar is, your ideas, and your overall vibe.

For example, you would not create a beauty product store if your followers love you because of your amazing fitness tips. It just doesn't jive.

You want to make your niche something that will be complimentary to your brand and fill a need for your avatar – otherwise your followers and customers will be confused and wonder why you are promoting something that they are not particularly interested in.

This is a quick way to lose trust and followers. You definitely do not want that.

You also want your niche to be fairly specific.

Is it your flawless skin that people are always complimenting you on? You may want to look into skincare products.

Do you have a rocking bikini body? You may want to focus on ab products.

Are you always holding a coffee? You may want to focus on different flavors/brands of coffee. The point is, find something you love!

Here is a mock-up of something you might create.

@darienfaith is a real girl – a natural beauty with a love for coffee. This is not a real post, but it is definitely something she could use. See how this works?

darienfaith • Following
Malibu

Enjoying this gorgeous day and my new favorite coffee flavor - Laguna from Coffee Joe! Great afternoon pick-me-up without the jitters. Love it!!  For all of you adventurous coffee drinkers, here is the link! www.bit.ly/dariens-favorites. #coffeefirst #afternooncoffee

Another thing to consider.

When you create your store, you will want to focus on just a few core products (start with just 3 or 4). Each of your products must be in the same product family. For example, you would not sell a hair dryer, eyelash curler and beach towel all from the same store. But, you would sell a beach towel, beach tote, and sand toys together.

Got some ideas? Awesome!

"There is never any hurry on the creative plane, and there is no lack of opportunity. . . the competitive mind is not the creative one."

--Wallace D. Wattles
The Science of Getting Rich

NAME YOUR STORE

Now that you have defined your niche and your avatar, you need to name your store. As an influencer, you know the importance of names and branding, so you want to make sure your store name will resonate with your customers.

Remember that simple is usually best.

Don't worry if you don't know exactly what you are going to sell in your store yet. It will come to you. There is plenty of time for you to research and test products before you recommend them.

This is not a race, my friend.

There is plenty of abundance for every person in this world. Try to stay on the creative side of things, and not the competitive side. You will find that as you stay creative and grateful, the ideas will come to you more frequently. You just have to put these ideas into action.

When you start to consider your store name, try a lot of different options.

Think of some online stores that you shop.

Stores like Away.com (luggage), Revolve.com (fashion), ClareV.com (handbags) have nice, simple, easy to remember names.

This is where you want to be. Try to avoid anything that sounds too kitschy.

Write down every idea that comes to you - even if you think it is silly. That silly name may inspire you to think of something else that will eventually lead to the name of your store.

Anything you write down at this point is just going to get your creative ideas flowing.

Now, look at the products themselves. Can you use the type of product as a name for your store? For example, if you were selling fitness products that helped build core muscles through balance products, you might jot down the name, corebalance or thebalancestore. Get the idea?

If you are going to focus on sunglasses, you could jot down some names like sunnies, sunspecs, or shades. These are just ideas to help you get to the next phase of finding your store name.

A good place to find potential store names is on Amazon – I mean, really, they do have everything. LOL.

Seriously, do a search for books that have something to do with your niche. A lot of thought has gone into these titles, and they are designed to grab the attention of potential readers. See if there is a word or two that pops out at you. Add these to your list.

The titles and names there might inspire you!

Another place to go is the Shopify Business Name Generator. Here is the link: https://www.shopify.com/tools/business-name-generator. This should give you a few more ideas.

Homework: Research possible names for your store. Make a list of 15-20 ideas.

See if you can take these words and mix them around or mash them together to make a new and better list.

Now, narrow down the list to your favorite 5-7. This is a good start.

WHO DO YOU TRUST?

Now is the time to get a second opinion. You have probably been looking at names for a while, researching, saying them out loud, writing them down, etc. This is like smelling too many perfumes.

You need a coffee bean. You need a good friend.

A few words about who you decide to share your vision with.

This person understands you and is excited for you! They are motivational and down to earth. They are uplifting and positive. They will listen to your ideas and brainstorm with you. They will want to share this moment with you!

It is very important that you do not bring your ideas to anyone who is going to shoot you down.

No need to bring in that potentially jealous co-worker who is going to find something bad to say about every one of your ideas. You need real discussion and suggestions here - not someone who is going to make you feel like a jackass for following your dreams.

Do you have that person? Good!

Now, see if you can take them out for coffee and ask if they would be willing to hear a few names for an online store that you are building. You will be surprised what collective intelligence can bring. If collective intelligence is positive and truly in tune with problem-solving, you will be blown away at how good it can get.

Try to narrow your selections down to your top 3 gems and put them in that order. The reason you need to do this is because your favorite may already be taken! You want to be sure that you can use the name to actually create your website – so you will need to check whether that particular domain has been taken.

You should also run these potential domain names through the following tests. You don't want to end up with a name that spells something inappropriate – you'd be surprised how easily this happens!

1. Say the domain name out loud and ask your friend to write it down. Can they spell it easily? (You want people to be able to find it).
2. Do the words spell anything strange?
3. Is it memorable?

Now let's see if the domains are available.

There are a bunch of different ways for you to check whether your store name is available. Services I have used in the past are NameCheap.com and GoDaddy.com, but there are so many that can do it for you!

My favorite lately is NameCheap.com. At NameCheap you can check to see if a domain is available and then you can buy it for a great price. NameCheap also sets up your domain name with privacy protections as part of their service.

Feel free to shop around and use any domain name service that you like best!

"Confidence isn't a function of how many affirmations you repeat each morning – but in how many steps you take in the path laid out in front of you."

--Amy Porterfield
Online Marketing Expert

THE FUN PART!

Now that you have a website name and a few cool product ideas, it's time to open up shop!

There are several e-commerce platforms you can use that are all very simple to set up. My favorite to use right now is Shopify. I have tried a few of the other ones, and although they work great, I found Shopify to be the easiest to get started with. Plus, it is easy to add apps that will make your store run better and provide opportunities to upsell.

A few other platforms that are available are Volusion and 3dCart. Feel free to try a few different options to see which is easiest for you to use.

Remember that you want to be able to integrate a dropshipping supplier into your store, so be sure that any e-commerce platform you pick has the ability to do that.

After trying a few different options, I found that Shopify is the most flexible, feature rich and most complete e-commerce platform of the many options available. Straight out of the box it has everything you may need to run a gorgeous and easy-to-use store. It also lets you customize your design as much as you would like to – and has all kinds of apps and helps to make your store freaking awesome.

You can sell just about anything you want to, including physical and digital products.

It also works great for dropshipping, which is what you will want to do.

I love that the goal of Shopify is to make it possible for anyone to easily launch their own e-commerce shop without having any design or technical skills.

You have nothing to lose! Shopify gives you a 14-day free trial period to get up and running, and after that it is only $29/month for the basic plan (which is all you need). You don't even have to give them credit card info to get started – you can totally just dive right in!

Click on the Free Trial and enter your name and email and then answer a few questions about whether it is your first time to start a store. These questions don't really matter, they just give Shopify an idea of whether you are a beginner or not.

Now you should be in!

Here are a few screen shots to get you started.

After you sign in and set up your shop, you will get to the welcome screen. This is your dashboard. Once your store starts making some sales, all of the daily information you will need will be right here!

Let's create your store.

Click on the Online Store button on the left side of the screen. And then click on Themes.

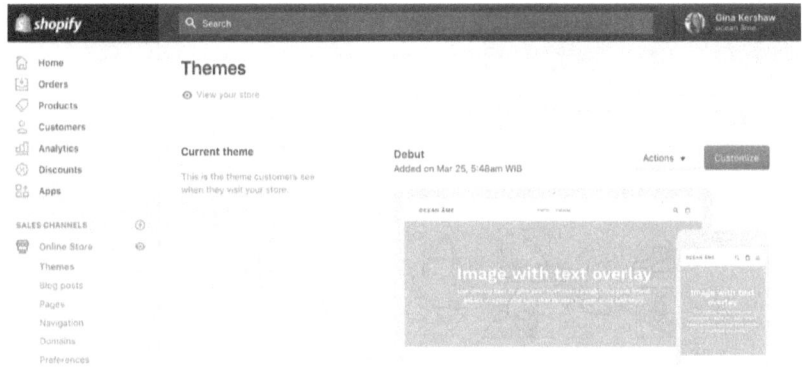

Have fun here you creative beast! There are a bunch of themes to pick from. There are plenty of beautiful free themes to use, or you may want something that is a bit more customized to your style.

Either way, pick a theme you love and then go to customize it. You will put your store name and other info into the theme to make it all yours. Amazing.

Now let's add in a few products.

Did you set up your AliExpress account? If you have not done that yet, go back to the Chapter about Shopping to set up an account and explore different product options.

You will definitely want to purchase a few of these items yourself before making them live on your shop. Remember that you will want to create your own photos and/or videos of the products you pick. But, for now, you are just going to try to put a few products in to learn the process.

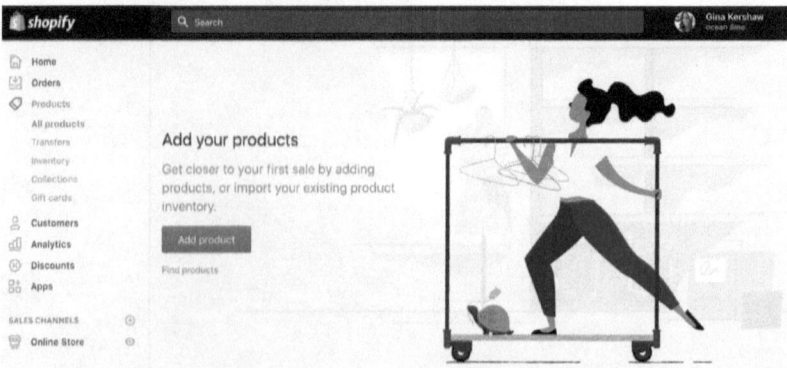

Go back to the main menu and click on "Products." This screen should come up! Now click on the "Find Products" link and this should take you to a screen that invites you to try Oberlo.

You definitely need Oberlo as an app for Shopify. This is the app that will attach AliExpress to your Shopify store. Follow all of the directions to add Oberlo as a Chrome Extension, and then connect your AliExpress account.

From this point on when you go to Ali-Express you will see a little blue tag that you can click on send the product right into your store! So easy!

Here is just a simple luggage tag as an example of what it looks like:

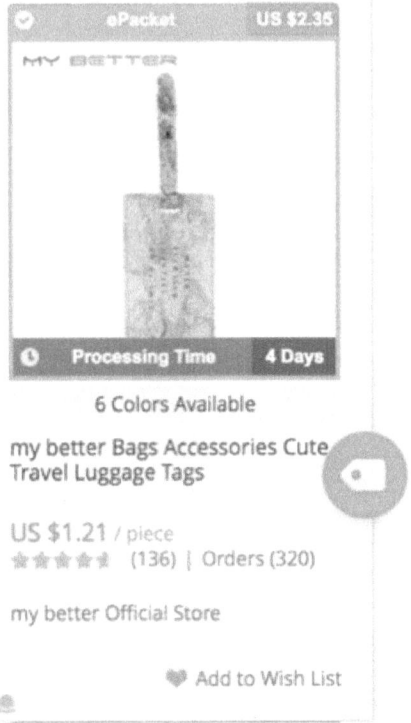

Remember how I showed you how to check how fast your product will ship? Notice that for this product, the "e-packet" green notification is at the top. This indicates you are using the fastest shipping.

Also notice that it has great reviews, and the price point is awesome!

The little blue tag that popped on the screen lets you know that Oberlo can import it right to your store.

Now you just need to customize the details.

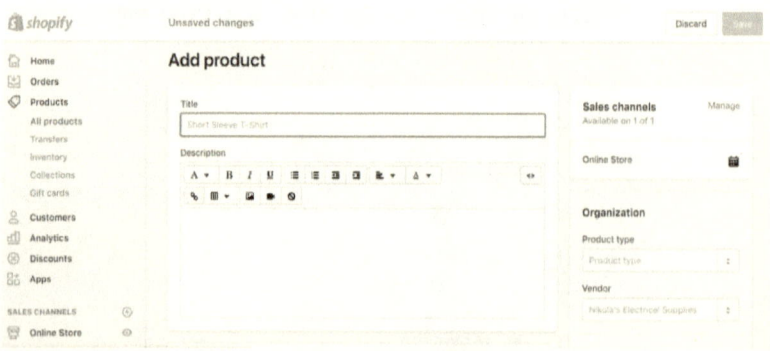

This is what the "Add Product" screen looks like.

You will want to come up with a really cool product name and description, add in a few photos, and then you want to make sure you set a price. You are almost there!!

After you have finished entering in your products, you will need to adjust some of the settings for your store.

Go to your settings screen to set up payment methods and checkout.

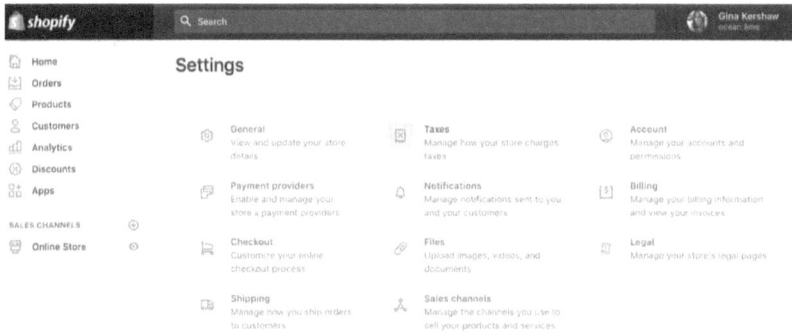

Take the time to go through each of these sections and make sure that everything is set up and ready to go. You want to make sure your money is coming in!!

Just a heads up on the "Legal" tab. I suggest that if you are serious about making this business successful and thriving that you set your store up legally.

By the way, going all in tells the universe you really are committed to your financial success, so I highly recommend you adopt this mindset!! If you set up the store without creating an official business (like a sole proprietor-ship or LLC), and you start having some kick-ass sales, Shopify will stop your payouts until your business is set up. This sucks.

Bottomline, go all in and do it right. Get some good business legal advice to set up the correct type of business. Check out LegalZoom for a fast way to get set up.

You are here and have read this far ... Yay! This means you really are serious about building your business smart and achieving all of those wealth and lifestyle goals you have.

Now you have the tools to make that happen!

LASTLY . . .

You are totally on your way to changing your life. I am so excited for you! Congratulations for having the courage to step outside your comfort zone, see your own amazing potential, and learn how to build your business smart. This new mindset is not only going to benefit your life in ways you always imagined, you are also going to have the knowledge to mentor and help others.

You can do this!

Remember that your unique personality and voice brought you to the place you are now. You have been able to build a following of people who admire you and who trust you. They enjoy your distinctive perspective on life, fashion, travel, fitness, etc.

You have something of value to offer, and you have people who want to hear about it!

Don't try to compete with anyone else. It doesn't matter how many other influencers and bloggers there are that may have the same type of account that you do. No one is exactly like you, and no one has the same exact followers that you do.

Try a little experiment.

Look up the Instagram account of another blogger that you compare yourself to. Look at how many followers you have in common. This should show you right now that the people that want to hear your voice and the people that want to hear her/his voice are not the same.

Yes, you may have some overlap, but for the most part, you each have different and unique qualities and things to offer. Realize that what you have to offer can only come from you – so stop comparing yourself and just go out there and do you!

The universe is more willing to bring you abundance when you focus on creativity and not competition. It knows that there is more than enough for everyone, so let it bless each individual as much as possible!

The contents of this book have given you a strong foundation to build your business smart.

Take it and run!

You have so much to offer the world, and the world has so much to offer you back. The future ahead of you can be filled with everything you have ever dreamed of. Take the opportunity to learn and make it happen.

This is your moment!

LET'S CONNECT

If you are serious about starting your online business, I recommend reading this book a few times and referring back to it when needed. You can also download a Free 21-Day Action Plan on my website www.ginakershaw.com to get started.

I can't wait to hear your stories about how you have taken steps to build your own influencer business! Let me know how you took your Influencer business to the next level and how your life is changing for the better! You can email me directly at InfluencerCEO@gmail.com.

Finally, PLEASE ☺ ... If you enjoyed this book, it would be amazing if you could leave a quick review on Amazon. It only takes a minute and would mean so much!!

Thank you so very much!

WORK WITH ME

Hi! I am Gina Kershaw - and, as you've probably guessed, teaching Bloggers how to use their influence to build a profitable business is what I love to do.

Just this year I helped one mom blogger go from not even knowing what e-commerce is ... to becoming an online business CEO who will bring in over $50K her first year. This is what makes my heart sing!

Using my 15+ years of experience in business with degrees in Finance, Marketing and Law (not to mention having owned my own business), I love to help women marry their creative talent with strategic smarts to build successful companies.

I've been where you are. I was a stay-at-home mom, and although I loved spending time with my children, I felt like I needed more. I needed my own identity (and my own money) again.

I know what you're thinking:

- What if I do all this work and no one buys anything?
- How the heck am I going to figure out this tech stuff with babies running around?
- And most importantly, who am I to be the CEO of a business?

Friend, who are you NOT to thrive in your life and business? This is for your personal growth, this is for your partnership, this is for your children. You standing in your expertise and power is so much bigger than an online store.

As for the details, that's where I come in! How would it feel to:

- have step-by-step guidance on figuring out the market that needs you, what products they're dying for and how you can best reach them?

- build your online store with an expert who can quickly and efficiently move you through the technical steps to get your business profitable in just 6 weeks!
- link arms with a fellow Mom for support in making your dreams come to fruition.

Have I mentioned that once your store is up and running you'll only need to invest 1 - 2 hours per week into maintaining and growing your company? A business that's open 24/7 and only requires a few hours a week of 'work' is just unheard of - but definitely not too good to be true!

I would love to chat with you about using your existing audience to create into a profitable e-commerce business! I look forward to meeting you!

www.ginakershaw.com/work-with-me

NOTES:

www.ingramcontent.com/pod-product-compliance
Lightning Source LLC
Chambersburg PA
CBHW021444210526
45463CB00002B/629